A Man Talks With God

A Man
Talks With God

BY

BOB W. PARROTT

Word Books, Publisher
Waco, Texas — London, England

To

DR. JOE BROWN

*a distinguished physician
and spiritual father of my ministry*

PREFACE

The talks in this book are not prayers of the traditional types (petition, intercession, praise, etc.). They are prayers in the sense that I talk to the Lord in an attitude and spirit of reliance upon Him.

So, for the sake of understanding what is happening in this book, we will shift our attention off the traditional prayer approach. And call these "talks" with God.

They are talks of involvement. When something struck me as a bit unusual, I wrote about it. And included "The Lord" in that involvement.

In the manner in which they are written, you might call them Christian happenings. As they happened, I wrote about them. Which in effect makes the book a kind of prayer diary.

This book is evidence of the fact that God reveals Himself to me through lives of others. What happens to them influences my life. And to some extent I am changed by lessons learned from their situations.

I hope that the reading of this book becomes an event in your life. Through which God reveals Himself to you. And that you become another person who talks with God.

My thanks to Dr. Charles L. Allen who for years through letters, phone calls, and personal visits has encouraged me to "keep on writing."

And to Mr. Bob Fry, parishioner and friend, who

helped me see "what the laymen wanted" and would never let me forget that I had to produce!

And to my patient, proof-reading secretary, Mrs. Joan Householder.

And to professor Doris Colbury, whose trained eyes caught those mistakes to which my own eyes had grown accustomed.

My final word of gratitude must be to my wife, who, second to the Lord, heard these talks. Her objective, critical remarks contributed much toward making this book what it is.

B. W. P.

CONTENTS

PART I
ABOUT ANXIOUS MOMENTS

1. The Fighter

In some ways, Lord, I suppose every man is a born fighter. But there are some things you can't fight.

Only this morning I saw the dilemma of every person in the face of an ex-professional boxer who had fought 173 fights and lost only three. This ex-commissioner of boxing in our state was standing with me by the hospital bedside of his wife. She was about to undergo surgery where cancer was suspected. Her boxer-husband clinched his fists until his knuckles turned white, tightened his lips into a thin line, and tears filled the eyes of his pugilistic face. If only he could catch his enemy, could see him, he'd surely knock him out.

But this fight he's caught up in is on the inside. It is a fight with fear, with uncertainty, with insecurity, with Death.

And it is a battle that he can only win with your help.

Keep him in your corner, Lord!

2. Guilt

Thank you, Lord, for guilt.
I remember the day I didn't have it. Well, maybe

I did, but I didn't recognize it.

Anyway, now I do have quite a capacity for that guilt feeling . . . a capacity born out of knowing my sin is forgiven.

What monsters we would be if we were unable to know guilt!

What horror monsters we are when we don't ask forgiveness!

Lord, give me a conscience, a sensitive conscience. Clobber me when I think only of myself. Guilt is a terrible feeling. But how much more terrible it would be not to feel guilt when I sin!

"Lord, be merciful to me a sinner."

Be merciful by making me guilty, by making me free of guilt, by giving me a conscience.

Mercy, how we need it!

3. *The Truth*

My Bishop says I can move this year, Lord, if I want to.

If *I want* to—if *I want* to.

It's not easy to explain my feelings to him or to you. But I'll try.

I've been at this pastorate for years. And you know what have been my ups and downs. I've been so disgusted at times that I'd have been willing to take a circuit on the moon. And yet I've had mountaintop experiences with my parishioners. The people whom I know and love the most are here. Here, Lord, in this community.

But then I know it's been this way wherever I've been

in these years of preaching. It's hard to say to the Bishop, "I want to leave."

So I practice my answers: "If a bigger challenge comes my way, I'll take it."

Maybe I should say: "I don't *want* to, and I want to. So I'll go."

Or: "I want to move, but don't tell my people because it would sound like I didn't want them."

Or: "I don't want to move, but I'm willing."

No, this smacks of untruth.

"If *you* want to," he says.

Why couldn't he put it some other way? I think I've discovered why. There's hardly any other way to put it.

So I said, "I'm ready to move, Bishop."

It feels better when you tell the truth, doesn't it, Lord?

4. Forgiveness

Undoubtedly one of the hardest truths to accept, Lord, is the truth of your forgiveness.

Over and over someone is asking, "How can I be sure I am forgiven?"

I can never quite adequately answer that question. Somehow I know better than to think I can answer it. But I keep trying.

I keep trying because at least my concern for their forgiveness may come through to them that this is your concern.

I do this because I am convinced that none other can forgive, save you.

And I am convinced that it is your will to forgive.

I tell them about your forgiveness because this is my

experience. I know I am forgiven. How can I convince others that really and truly our unconditional surrender to you puts us in a position to receive forgiveness?

No working for it, no getting good, no being sweet, no self-image of worthiness—nothings gets us forgiveness. Your grace is sufficient.

Oh, Lord, we believe. Help us in our unbelief.

5. *War Is Hell*

In so many ways, Lord, war is hell. The hell is obvious in the suffering of injury and death. But war carries along a thousand other agonies. Some we don't recognize. Which makes the futility of it all more tormenting.

Only this morning I listened to a world traveler, who is a journalist, tell of his efforts to help 300,000 children born of Korean mothers and American GIs. Also after trips to Vietnam he has visited the Pentagon in trying to seek help for the 40 babies born out of wedlock every week to Vietnamese women and American GIs.

To hear of what was being done to help these nameless children warmed my heart.

But a chill came over me when the speaker said to a small private gathering later: "We aren't against the soldiers having fun; we just want the pill made available."

"We aren't against the soldiers having fun . . ."

War is hell, Lord.

6. *Temptation*

I am tempted to fill a fellow pastor in on all the petty details concerning a man who recently left our fellowship for his.

This man and his wife claimed to be tithers while they were in our church. And were relatively "happy" for a few years in the church. That is, for the years the man had a position of top leadership in the church. And then following his replacement, he began to find little things wrong with what his successor was doing. Until finally he said some very unkind words to his successor. Alienation by choice was taking place. Then they threatened moving if the same counselor stayed in the youth division over their children. Then they didn't like the manner in which the offerings were counted. Then finally they moved their membership . . . and made it known that they will never tithe again because of the way things had gone at our church!

Obviously they never were tithers in spirit. And all this maneuvering was a most dishonest way to find a scapegoat for their decision to quit giving as much to the church.

And I am tempted to tell all about them.

But since it is a temptation, I know it's the devil pushing me. And not you, Lord.

I learned a long time ago that Paul was right. You never tempt man. You only love us. And love invites us to do good, motivates us to "be kind one to another, tenderhearted, and forgiving one another."

And it would not be love that would cause me to talk about this man to his new pastor. I could tell all the truth about him and still be wrong.

It surely helps to know that any temptation to do anything makes the action automatically wrong. This is one truth I want to remember:

"A man must not say when he is tempted, 'God is tempting me.' For God cannot be tempted by evil, and does not himself tempt anyone."   Phillips. 1:13

7. *Hiding*

Recently I watched a bee attempt to make a home for himself in the tube opening which measures airspeed on my plane.

And then again I was awakened in our cabin among the rolling hills of East Texas by the fluttering of birds' wings as they were seeking shelter down the chimney.

Why is it, Lord, that crawling, flying, squirming things seek out holes?

I don't know about these other creatures. But I know about myself. That old hole-hunting urge comes when I blunder socially. Like the time I opened the door to a home after hearing a distinct "come in" from the inside—only to find the lady of the house frantically running for proper clothing. It was her parrot bird which issued the invitation, not she!

I get that hole-hunting feeling when I have miserably failed. Failed to get just the right word over to a family that is breaking up. They go their separate ways and I never hear from them again—When I have failed to be the success I think I ought to be.

I look for that hole when I've sinned. Mostly this hole-hunting remains an urge. I know it won't work. I've tried it. I just can't find a hole that hides me. You're always there, Lord, peeking in and bidding me to come on out— Out into the same world that drives me to the hole. Into a world of pressures and competition where I can make mistakes. But where you, Lord, help me learn from them. Into a world where I can sin. But where you, Lord, will forgive me.

I suppose we all have times that we feel like going somewhere to hide, Lord. We cannot stop the urge. But we can keep ourselves from going there. We can with your help, Lord.

It's a simple prayer. But it expresses what we feel: "Keep us out of holes, Lord, out of the smallest depression."

8. Problems

Every time I'm inside the Domed Stadium here in Houston, I am staggered by its mammoth size. A baseball field plus 45,000 seats under one roof. A roof so high that the strongest batter can't come near hitting it with a ball.

But then, every time I fly my plane over the city, the stadium resembles more a contact lense. It is so small.

My problems look much the same way. When I am in them, they tend to overpower me with their staggering proportions.

But then, Lord, when you get me out and above them, their dimensions are less pondersome.

If I know the pattern of my life, one day I will again feel flattened by circumstances beyond my control. But to stay true to that pattern of my life's history, your faith in me will carry me soaring above all obstacles.

That, Lord, is where I am today. I will come down into the world of problems whenever you feel I should.

But, if you can, let me stay up awhile longer!

9. *Real Parents*

Lord, I learn as much from those who come to me for counsel as they ever get from me.

What I learned from this young woman is a lesson for everybody.

Being an adopted child, she had not known the mother who gave her birth. For twenty years she had lived with and loved her adoptive parents. Then out of the black of the night a telephone call told her that her mother was in a hospital.

The young lady said, "You have the wrong party. My mother is here at home with me and doing very well."

The party on the other end of the line answered: "No, I'm not talking about the one you are living with. I'm talking about your real mother."

When the young woman called me and told me this story, her dilemma was obvious. She asked, "Who is my real mother?"

At this point I learned the lesson when I in turn asked, "Whom do you consider your real mother?"

To which she answered, "I don't even know this woman who claims to be my mother. She is a complete stranger to me. My mother is the one who raised me, gave me a home, and loved me."

At the end of our conversation she said, "For years I wondered who my real mother was. Now I know. She's been with me all the time."

In this case I saw that being a mother is more than having a baby. Motherhood is earned.

I realized that I am not a father just because I have a child. I am a father only if my daughter recognizes that quality in me.

And more, too. I am a pastor, not because I am sent to a church. I am a pastor when the people accept me as such.

I am not a husband just because the marriage license says so. I am a husband only when my wife recognizes this in me.

And now, Lord, I see that I am not your child just because I am human. As a human I am a created creature of yours. But I am your child because I have chosen to be. *I* want to be. I want to be your child any way you'll have me. Being adopted is just fine.

But we "have received the Spirit of adoption, whereby we cry, Abba, Father."

I don't wonder who my real Father is. You've been with me all the while.

10. *The Red Velvet Cake*

Lord, there's got to be a lesson in here somewhere. Where, so help me, I don't know. But let's talk about it. And see where this leads us.

My wife baked two layers for a Red Velvet cake, carefully wrapped and froze them for this very special vacation at our retreat in East Texas. On the day before we were to leave, she spent an hour preparing the icing and putting on the finishing touches. Carefully placing the cake in a tupperware container, she nursed it on the plane all the way to touchdown. Till that moment the beautiful cake had received more kindly attention than anybody on board.

Then I took over. Unthinking, I transferred the cake to the waiting auto's back of the back seat. Where plenty of sun could hit it. And it hit it all right. When my wife asked where the cake was, and I told her, I could tell by the look on her face that I had done something drastically wrong!

That melted cake overflowed the cake plate and settled to a smooth level in the tupperware container. And the smell was atrocious.

As we stared into that sight, it was awful, Lord. Not the cake so much as the way I felt. I won't even try to describe that strange awful feeling.

All that work and preparation in shambles, by one innocent act of ignorance.

I suppose that in every great accomplishment in the world, there is someone around who can ruin it.

If they should do this unintentionally, that is bad. But it is much worse when the destruction is intentional.

And there's my redemption in this case. It was an unintentional blunder.

Finally, we can live in a world of unintentional blunders without lingering effects because we know there is no attitude in that blunderer that would destroy us.

It's those intentional sinners, Lord, that really tear us up. It's the knowledge that some would willfully destroy our best efforts that keep us shaken up.

Others' mistakes may hurt us temporarily. We had better watch out if others' mistakes keep us hurt. With that attitude we could hurt somebody willfully. And lose our own souls.

I felt in the beginning there was a lesson in that minor trauma. And there was. I've described it.

But I also learned something else. I learned not to put cakes in the hot sun!

PART II
ABOUT SOCIAL EVENTS

11. Sanity

The state of affairs in the world is bad, Lord, real bad. We have obvious enemies who would destroy us if they could. Un-civilization is all around us.

But today something happened which shows that our nation has not drowned herself in morbid fears, irrational thinking, and hatred propaganda. A level of maturity was expressed when all over America people in shocked grief mourned the death of Russia's cosmonaut Komarov.

We honestly grieve over the loss of an enemy who only hours before his death praised the atheistic, communist regime of his homeland. This is close to, if not actually loving our enemies and praying for those who despitefully use us.

Keep us sane like that, Lord. In defending our country we don't want to lose our souls.

12. Easter Morning

Lord, it's Easter morning. And the church sanctuary is filled to overflowing. You see it.

What are they here for, Lord?

Behind those frilly dresses and flowery bonnets are

11

souls of people whom I see caught up in the life-and-death struggle of just existing.

I don't have to tell them there is death. They know it; they feel it in loneliness and despair.

So I will talk with them about life—in the here-and-now and after death. I will talk with them about you who are "the resurrection and the life."

They like that kind of talk, Lord. But do they really believe it?

       ❂   ❂   ❂

It's the Sunday following Easter, Lord. And one-half of the Easter crowd believed . . .

13. Writing

The time of the day has arrived which I had previously allotted for writing. And I just sit here in a private study where no ringing telephone is heard, with pencil in hand, blank paper galore, reference books scattered all around me—and nothing happens! Here I am in the midst of what some would call a perfect writing environment. And nothing happens!

I'm leaving. . . .

       ❂   ❂   ❂

Well, I'm back. And as enthused as a little boy just home from an exciting, adventurous movie. In this state of mind writing seems so easy, so natural. I've just got to talk to somebody!

After visiting with a tough, husky longshoreman and his wife and hearing how they both felt deeply the need of Christian worship and living, how they have through you discovered a love for each other that they have never known, I have been pushed off dead center. Their witness triggers me to say, "Thanks, Lord. Thanks for everything."

And I've discovered a truth in it all. I can't write until there's something to write about. And what is there to write about except life?

It just might be that the great writers didn't hide to write . . . that they exposed themselves to life's delights, and wrote in response to those experiences.

14. Coming of Age

I read where some say that modern man "has come of age," that he is self-sufficient and does not need you to lean on, Lord. It must be a godly feeling to think one is strong enough to whip any problem. I am scared of a man who feels this way. He could hurt somebody and think he is doing "man" a favor.

I've thought about this "coming of age" bit. It applies to my life this way. I am just at the age that I know you are my Father. Of all your children, I am the weakest. That's why I pray so much for strength.

Your power helps me to accept my inadequate self and understand my weak brothers. I find myself in situations every day that would cause me to lose faith in my brothers without your undergirding insight of "there but for the grace of God go I." When a drunken woman curses me, when a committee member stomps out in disgust, when a tither quits tithing, when a minister throws his wife aside for the affections of another, when a priest gets drunk at a football game, when two church members of the same congregation won't speak to each other, when preachers are jealous of who got what church, and when members of churches are jealous over who gets the jobs in the churches . . . I tend to grow weary. Then I realize that if I let that tendency overtake me, I have joined that crowd.

I have "come of age" Lord. I am just old enough to know I need a forgiving Heavenly Father.

If I should live to become a helpless old man, too weak to walk, too far removed from that generation to care, I shall be then where I am now: a small weak child crying for the comfort and strength of its Heavenly Parent.

15. Integration

Integration . . . what is it, Lord?

It's bound to be more than granting races equal rights to public facilities, than forcing a company to hire employees according to the race's ratio of the population, than letting a man of another race sit in "our" church. Where in all cases we are so conscious of what we have done in creating integration.

According to the definition of some, maybe this is integration.

But I had an experience recently that won't let me settle for such superficial "integration." I was visiting in prison with three men, two negroes and one Mexican. After hearing each of them agonize over their own sin against you, Lord, I unthinkingly put my left arm around the broad, black shoulders and my right arm around the thin little brown shoulders . . . and prayed for all of *us*.

Two negroes, one Mexican, and a white man together in prayer. We were integrated and didn't know it, Lord.

But isn't that, after all, the Christian definition of the word?

After that jailhouse experience, any less "integration" seems too, too little.

16. *The Comforter*

What a Comforter you are Lord!

Following a funeral service this morning for a sixty-eight year old man who never professed you as Lord, yet profaned your name often, a member of the family who appeared to be a concerned Christian said to me: "I always wondered what could be said by a minister at the funeral of such a man."

And my answer was: "It's really very simple. I try to comfort the living."

Hit us with the truth, Lord! Who are we to judge anybody who has died? You said that you would "come again" in sending the Comforter. And I can vouch that you do "come again" and again through the minister whose primary aim in such an occasion is to comfort.

This good news can joyfully be proclaimed in any "difficult" situation.

17. *Knowing Each Other*

We've been back to the prison unit, Lord. I learn something from every trip.

But this time I saw a dimension of soul I had never seen before.

The men listened intently as one of our "big-name preachers" witnessed. When he mentioned that he knew the God who created the thousands of acres which was the prison farm, that he, personally loved the soil, the trees, the cattle—the inmates believed him. They were visibly moved by his prayers.

They were moved because this man was moved. It was the dimension of soul in that preacher that caught my attention.

Those prisoners did as much for him as he did for them.

But after all, Lord, isn't that so with all of us?

It's others, their needs, and you, your will, that brings the best out of any of us.

I especially enjoyed that trip. I saw my friend like I had never seen him before.

. . . You know, Lord, I'm wondering if he is saying the same thing about me.

18. Poverty

Lord, I could hardly believe my eyes when I visited the place of your childhood, Nazareth in the Galilee country of Palestine. Could it be that you really lived in a cave, slept in the same quarters as the milch goats and donkeys, and used water from a common well that served the entire village?

My Lord, if you did, and they say you did, you lived in conditions of poverty that would be worthy of the investment of the largest Federal grant. In these days we feel a moral obligation to help people better an environment that in cases is superior to yours.

We need your guidance as to how to do it. You went about doing good in a different way. You healed the maimed, the blind by touching their spirits with your spirit. On every turn you fought the poverty of the spirit . . . with the Samaritan woman at the well, with Nicodemus, with the temple priests, with Herod Antipas, with Pontius Pilate, with the two thieves on the crosses— with everybody you knew.

Help us, Lord, that we will not drop your primary values of the spirit for secondary ones. With your spirit we won't forget that secondary values are still *values!* And we'll do something about them.

19. *Comforting*

There is no doubt that one of the greatest testing times for a pastor is during a death situation. As you notice, Lord, the more the people tend to depend on me in those times, the weaker I feel, and the more I depend on you! When people look to me for comfort, I turn to the Comforter . . . you!

I accept each of those situations as serious challenges. But a few of them, Lord, leave me limp. I try hard, but just don't seem to get through.

For instance, when the young widow requested my help in selecting the casket for her deceased husband, I tried to inform her that the funeral was not for show. What did she do? She chose a funeral service that would make sure the neighbors wouldn't talk about her "not putting her husband away proper like."

Then she had trouble accepting the mortician's work. Finally I convinced her that he "looked natural."

Then we had to pick a grave site. It was decided that the body would be buried where the man wanted. But it was hard to decide where he would have wanted since he was dead.

At that point the family fell apart. One sister said one place, the wife said another; the wife had her way, and the family in general became unhappy with each other. On the day of the burial, some wouldn't even speak to each other.

After the benediction at the graveside and the service was concluded, one I know for sure was comforted—me! It was over!

And, Lord, I'm wondering if I did too good a job at comforting the widow, and encouraging her to live on. In five months she was married again!

Let's face it, Lord. I'm just human. And cannot finally comprehend how your redemptive grace works in such mismanagement. So I'm not going to give it another thought. Except to say . . . I'll do my best at the next grief situation. I'll continue to call on you. And trust that things will turn out better than my mind is able to comprehend.

PART III
ABOUT UNUSUAL SITUATIONS

20. Strong Talk

Lord, I want to thank you for patience that helps me listen to troubled souls. This in itself provides a kind of therapy for their miserable spirits.

But for some situations this obviously is not enough. Some people's temperament demands a bit of aggressive witnessing. Thanks to you, Lord for the courage to speak out and the wisdom to know when to speak.

There was such an occasion I shall never forget. A man came to me seeking counsel concerning his shaky marriage. I spent my time listening until he came up with a written list of the things his wife had done that irritated him.

When I asked the reason for the list, he answered, "That's so I won't forget what makes me so mad."

I first thought the man was joking. But he wasn't.

And I wasn't either when I told him that with an attitude like that no woman in her right mind could live with him.

And she didn't.

He later remarried. And again came to me as the troubles set in. This time I hit him hard, real hard, with his obvious sins. Recalling how he had driven his pre-

vious wife away. And emphasizing that it was happening
all over again.

Only you know, Lord, whether this straightforward
reprimand helped or not.

But we both know that I didn't hurt their marriage.
It's been seven years now, and the family has been
welded together in a spirit that was not there.

I believe that spirit is your spirit.

And as I recall, it was in that spirit that I spoke to him.

21. Pastors

Every now and then I see the church functioning as it
ought, with some of its members being the pastors of
others. Now I am not boasting of their goodness, only
you are good, Lord. Anyway, this is what they are supposed to be . . . pastors.

But this particular situation so vividly relates the pastoral role that Christians are supposed to play for others.

It happened something like this, Lord:

A man got out of prison.

A Christian family of the community took this stranger
into their home.

They found him a job; he rented an apartment, called
his young wife to come to him from eastern United States.
Now he, she, and the baby are united and happy.

Many people would be skeptical about the possibili-
ties of that family staying together. And I'll admit that
a criminal record, an illiterate young wife, and the added
financial responsibility of a baby would make this marriage look like a poor risk on the surface.

But they have a chance, no, more than a chance. They

have all the opportunity in the world to make a "go of it." Opportunity provided by a dozen pastors.

You've seen these pastors' concern for the down-and-out family. Indeed, you've seen them. You put them there, Lord! While this trouble-struck family has attended our church and heard my sermons, I accept as a fact that any one of these dozen has been a more effective pastor than I for these poor, dear people. In fact I hesitate to do or say too much. These pastors are doing such a grand job on their own.

The proof of this came for me on the night that they all met at the young struggling family's apartment. And talked about you, Lord, for two hours! My status there was more of an observer. And I appreciated that role. I saw concerned Christians doing what they are supposed to do, being what they are called to be—pastors!

You know, Lord, if I had a few more associate pastors like these, we could turn this community upside down . . . Uh, oh, now I get the point. Those are your plans!

22. *Christian Understanding*

My thinking was wrong.

Southern Baptists are not way out there in right field by themselves. Proud to be alone, looking down their noses at mainstream denominations.

Why, indeed, I've found that I've got some Baptist "blood" in me. Maybe the Baptists have got Methodist "blood" in them. I notice they have numerous Wesley hymns in their hymnal!

No, it must be that we all have you, Lord, way down deep in our souls. And we felt it last night in Dialogue with the local Baptist minister in their auditorium.

In that discussion we learned that it really amounted to little whether the worship is in an "auditorium" or a "sanctuary." Whether baptism was "in" water or "with" water. Whether the Lord's Supper was a "sacrament" or whether it was simply "The Lord's Supper."

We learned that we were blood brothers in your body in this world, Lord. We found we were both evangelical in history, past and present. That what mattered most was that we all accept you as Lord of our lives. Who has accepted us in spite of our sin by the saving act of forgiving us.

I'm still scratching my head about the Dialogue. It surely seemed like they loved me and accepted me as one of their own.

You got to me through them. I hope you used me in the same way to get through to them.

Somehow I have the feeling you did.

Talking with and understanding each other is good for our souls. I know. This is what I've gotten through this little talk with you . . . a touch of goodness.

23. Knowing You

My Lord, what a conversation! After talking four hours with a NASA physicist, my brain's in a whirl. It's past 12:00 midnight. And there's no rest.

What has that guy done to me?

I know what he's done. He made me think.

But I know what I've done. I made him think.

To his initial statement, "I can't see how God could die when I don't believe he's ever been alive," I answered: "you are right; God is not alive." And he very nearly fainted. Those of us who know you personally as Heavenly Father know that you are more than living stuff that physics deals with. We know that you live, in our hearts, motivating us, healing us, loving us.

Nobody "won" that conversation. We both learned from the other. But he listened very intently as I witnessed my firm faith in your gift of eternal life. Evidently this bothered his scientific mind. But undoubtedly he remains fascinated with the possibility.

* * * * * *

He came into the church Sunday. From within the fellowship our conversations will continue, and we will learn more. Our ideas about the nature of your Being may change. But our knowledge of what you've done for us will never change. Those personal experiences are what made us sit up and take notice of you. It is the witness of those experiences that make others sit up and take notice of you.

As followers of your way in Christ Jesus, help us to give what people will listen to. Help us to witness the impact that you have made on our lives, Lord. And may your spirit of Truth redeem that witness in order that inquiring minds will hear with their hearts the full import of what is being said about you.

24. Honky Tonk Angel

Everywhere I go, I find you've been there, Lord.

And I have concluded that no place is so secular that you cannot squeeze in.

This was brought home to me during my last visit to a maximum security unit of our state's penal system. Six barred doors along corridors were unlocked to let our small party into an auditorium, where we were the only audience for a dozen inmates who were on the stage playing musical instruments and singing. It was their recreation period.

The song which impressed me with the truth of your presence everywhere was titled, "I Didn't Know God Made Honky Tonk Angels." The man who sang this song performed as if he were the one who made this discovery. And looked like he'd been in enough Honky Tonks to know of what he was singing!

If ever a place is dedicated to the Devil, it's the Honky Tonk. But even there you are. Else why would the writer and the singer of this song even mention you? Now that "Honky Tonk Angel" might well be another man's wife, the barmaid, or a prostitute. But the point the singer brought home to me was that he loved her. And unconsciously (since you were passively mentioned) admitted that you were the Creator of love. As immoral as she might have been, and as immoral as he was (his crime had to be of the worst for him to have been where he was), he could love and sense that this love is your gift to man.

Psalms 139:7-12

Whither shall I go from thy spirit? or whither shall I flee from thy presence? If I ascend up into heaven, thou art there, if I make my bed in hell, behold, thou art there. If I take the wings of the morning, and dwell in the uttermost parts of the sea; even there shall thy hand lead me, and thy right hand shall hold me. If I say, Surely the darkness shall cover me; even the night shall be light about me. Yea, the darkness hideth not from thee; but the light shineth as the day: the darkness and the light are both alike to thee.

—Amen.

25. *The Flunker*

Lord, how can you help a boy like this? He's a graduating senior in high school. But he's flunking out at home. He has convinced himself that he can never be happy at home.

I've tried to help.

I've tried to talk with him . . . with his parents.

And remember, Lord, the times that we all talked with you about the problems.

After the morning's session a week ago, it seemed that there was some real progress.

I thought we had it made.

And then last night the door bell rang at a late hour. And there he was . . . standing in the door.

"I just know I can never be happy at my home," he told me, Lord.

And I just know I have miserably failed in all my counseling with him.

But come to think of it, Lord. He did come back to *my* doorbell. He came back and told *me* that *I* had not helped him find a place in his home.

Send him back again, Lord. I'm reaching him!

26. *W. S. C. S.*

My Lord, what am I going to do with my Woman's Society of Christian Service? They're at it again.

And I don't mean that they are "at" the business of spreading good news. They are "at" each other's throats. It's over a cook book. Or something like that.

My role in this particular situation is more like a referee between two teams than a pastor of a flock.

Nobody really won the battle at the meeting I attended. Each side's I-won't-budge-an-inch attitude made it a stand-off.

Could this be the true picture of the church as it is: a battle ground?

Could it be that the church is not so much in the world as the world is in the church?

Maybe this is not the way things *ought* to be, Lord, but when I take them the way they *are*, there's less frustration when I have to be the referee. And much joy when I am privileged with being their pastor.

Today, I'm pastor. At my suggestion, they are side by side ministering to a mother and children whose husband and father was taken in death yesterday morning.

I could not by myself get enough food there for all the folks of the deceased; I could not baby-sit with the children; I could not stay hour after hour and do the thousand-and-one things that these ladies did for the grief-stricken family.

Lord, what would I do without my Woman's Society of Christian Service?

27. *And He Was Just A Man*

Lord, I'm having the bishop of our area to preach for me this coming Sunday morning. And then he and his wife are to have dinner in our home.

What I want to ask is: how do you act around a bishop? What kind of man is he? What do you do when you've "got" a bishop?

And you've heard the inward groanings of my wife. Oh, she hasn't said a word to me. But I know what she's asking: what do they like in the way of the main dinner course, breads, desserts? Do I keep my house in an order equal to hers?

Questions, questions . . . we've got them, Lord.

* * * * * *

It's the day after, Lord. And you've given me the answers to my questions. Like always, you've "answered" me through experience.

I had the bishop. And discovered that he was just a man like myself.

He was such an ordinary person that he made *me* feel at home. He was a friend.

Now I know what makes a man great. It is a Spirit of love that makes you feel accepted and needed.

Through a man I've discovered the Greatest.

28. *A Greasy-Looking Character*

I sat where they sat. And, Lord, it hurt.

I was taking advantage of the warm Gulfcoast sunshine by combining work with pleasure. The work was the changing of oil in my Beechcraft Bonanza airplane. And the pleasure was the being out of "preachers clothes."

It usually takes quite a while to get the job done. Well, not really. But when I watch every teeny puddle jumper as well as every monstrous jet take off and land between each turn of the wrench, time surely gets by in a hurry. It's real fun.

And then I remembered. I was supposed to call the president of our neighborhood bank and tell him that I would be able to be his guest at a Rotary luncheon and have part on the program. Time was a'wastin'. Because in two hours I was to be there.

Dropping my tools and hastily washing my hands, I rushed over to the luxurious lounge of a large oil company's hangar. And walked up to a secretary and asked, "Could I use your phone?" She looked at me as if I had the plague and turned to what I suppose was her boss who had heard my question. And then he looked at me like she had looked at me. Only he had scorn on his face.

And then I realized what was wrong. I was not dressed "like a preacher." Quite the contrary, I was a sweaty, greasy-looking character with a torn T-shirt, faded blue jeans, and what were supposed to be white tennis shoes.

After a long look down his nose at me, the man nodded in a manner that suggested, "use it and get gone."

Anyway, that's what I did.

What a lesson that was for me, Lord. Any time I see "that greasy-looking character," I am offering him "a cool cup of water" in your Spirit.

29. *The Apollo Flight*

I don't feel that it's too early, Lord, for us to start praying for the success of the next Apollo mission.

I mean to start praying for the workers who inspect every rivet, every wire, every spring, every handle, every filament. They need to be "prayed for" as much as the astronaut. On their concern and workmanship the lives of the astronauts depend.

This absolute fact was brought home to me this week. Stepping into the Apollo simulator at NASA, I flew co-pilot with Donn Eisele on a rendezvous mission with a target which hypothetically carried stranded astronauts.

Bumping the thrusters, Donn got us within two miles of the target.

And then it happened. The computer went crazy.

In the real situation, we would have sailed past the target and the lives it contained would have been left behind forever.

The possibility of that happening scared me enough that I want to start praying now . . .

Guide them, Lord, all of them . . . riveters, engineers, machinists, electricians, sheet metal workers, photographers, theorists, physicians, astronauts. Amen.

Footnote: Donn Eisele, astronaut assigned to this nation's next Apollo flight, is a member of Seabrook Methodist Church.

30. Your Acceptance

Lord, do you really accept me when I do crazy things, silly things, stupid things? It seems rather appropriate that you are approvingly smiling upon my efforts as I give it all I've got in preaching, in visiting, in studying, in administering the affairs of the church.

But how do you feel when I am the bumbling fool?

To be specific, how do you feel about the night I was resting in the big den chair. And Doris came in with a piece of pie. Which I immediately knocked off the arm of the chair onto the floor. Then in getting up to clean up the mess, I bumped her elbow. And all over the floor her pie spilled. It was enough to bring us near tears.

How do you look at such a bumpkin who is supposed to be a leader, to be in control of the situation?

. . . I get the feeling you must be grinning, Lord.

31. *Life On Other Planets*

My scientist friends here in spaceland tell me they are convinced there's life on other planets. They say that there are billions of planets whose atmospheres can support life forms.

Lord, these men have more faith that this is true than I do. It must be faith that makes them believe this "fact" because nobody has been there to prove conclusively that there is life.

It makes me feel kind of strange, saying scientists have more faith than I, a minister. But in regards to this matter of whether there's life out there on other planets, they believe it with all their souls.

But don't count out my own faith, Lord, . . . in you! I personally am saying there can certainly be life on other planets . . . if you want life there!

Just because the earth had an atmosphere that could support life did not automatically mean that life was here. That extra bit of creation was up to you.

I strongly suspect that you've put life elsewhere in the universe. If you have, it changes nothing between us and you. We will still be sinners in the need of forgiveness.

The only change will be in our amount of knowledge of the universe. And that's already changing in leaps and bounds. When life for a certainty is discovered in those far away places, it will simply mean a whopper of a leap-and-bound.

But, Lord, I'm concerned. What if we don't get along with that life any better than we have each other here?

This would be a tragic discovery if we should use that life as a means of continuing destruction.

My concern is yours, Lord. Somewhere along the way we have lost our sense of priorities. First, we need you in our lives here, that whatever life we may discover "out there" will not be contaminated, but will be transformed by our touch.

Wherever we go on this earth or in this universe, we want to go with your good will.

Recreate within us that new spirit, Lord. Begin with me!

32. Eating Words

What's come over me, Lord?

Things I once didn't like to do, now I'm thrilled at doing. When I was a boy I would stare up at the sun from a rose, potato, or tomato field and swear that if I ever got out of that mess, I'd never look at the country again.

And this morning I found myself in a hot, sandy field picking peas!

Why do we spend a vacation in the country I once despised? Maybe the pleasure comes in knowing I don't have to do this! That's partly it. But a bigger reason for the relaxation in the country is the break it provides in the normal rush, rush of an urban ministry.

There's no telephone here. Only one car has passed by all day. And it didn't even honk a horn.

Someone once said:

> Be careful of the words you say,

To keep them soft and sweet,
You never know from day to day
Which ones you'll have to eat.

Lord, regarding those bitter words about the country I said years ago . . . I've gladly eaten them. I was never so wrong. Which reminds me, Lord. If I should gripe about some so-called hardship now, slap me across the face with the truth. That "hardship" might be a blessing.

PART IV
ABOUT CHRISTIAN ASPIRATIONS

33. A Witness

I have come to realize a truth that really thrills me, Lord.

After preaching for years, after a bachelor of Divinity in Theology, after many insights into how you work in this world . . . I have discovered that the best way to win people to you is to witness to them of what you have meant to me. That witness has shaken intellectual giants. It has brought college professors, physicians, technicians, engineers, to their knees.

Oh, my theologizing about you has tickled their fancy. And has in some respects gained me a foothold inside their heart's door. But after my theological chirping gets their attention, my abiding belief in your power wins them.

No, not always does it win them. They won't let it at times. But that witness always makes them think. It makes them think thoughts on a different level than the theological games of batting thoughts back and forth.

Our personal experiences with you speak louder and clearer than do mental gymnastics about you. And people listen. Where arguments may twist them over to our side, a witness can convert them to your way of life.

This realization accounts for those many, many prayers from me which ask for direct help from you, Lord. When you've got me, the people get the message. Without you nobody hears anything.

34. *Where We Stand*

Science has taught me much about you, Lord.

At one time we thought that our earth was the center of the universe. Then science corrected that when we learned that we revolved around the sun, thus putting the sun at the center. Now we are told that we are traveling around a sun which itself is at the extreme edge of our galaxy. And we are comfortable in the knowledge that we finally know where we are.

But Lord, have we really learned where we stand in this vast universe?

Why can't we see ourselves where we really are? Our position in this fantastically expanding universe is one relative, not to just heavenly bodies we see, but to an infinite universe. And to the infinite creator of it all. To you!

This is where science has led me. My stance in this vast, vast universe is relative to Infinity, to you.

My life had a beginning. And it will have an end. But I have the feeling, no, I have the faith, that you will "Expand" my life beyond the galaxy, beyond the universe, beyond thought-capability, into infinity. The lifetime of a star will be as nothing in comparison to that life with you.

35. *Love Does Strange Things*

Lord, I can't understand how she puts up with such a rotten husband.

This lady told me that her estranged husband was living with another woman, that he comes by once or twice a week and relates his experiences with his playmate, that he can't see how he can do without either of them . . .

This man is walking all over her. Which normally would seem to be enough to warrant her to jump free of his grasp. But she says that in spite of all this wretched treatment, she loves him!

As her counselor, I stated that if anybody had just cause to divorce her husband, she did—that it was beyond my understanding how she could put up with such injustice.

And then I realized that you were working in her life. And that this is how you work in this world of people. Your love is always beyond our understanding. You accept the unacceptable, love the unlovable, redeem the unredeemable. That is the kind of love she has toward her wayward husband.

Stay with her, Lord. And I'll be sure not to interfere with what you are doing.

36. *I Judged*

Woe is me, Lord. I did it again. I judged.

The phone rang this A.M. and the disinterested funeral home secretary's voice droned out the death message. A member of my flock had died.

I guess you could call him a member of my flock. His

name was on the books. But the only times I saw him were when he was hospitalized with illness. He surely seemed to like to see me then!

When I got the death message, I reacted like the human you keep telling me I am. I turned to a minister friend visiting with me in my office and said, "I know where that old boy is right now. He got used to Hell before he died. He was a scoundrel if I ever saw one."

Actually, Lord, I considered the man worthless.

And then I drove up to the home. And was met by a little teary eyed, eight-year-old, red-headed boy who slipped his arm around my neck and cried, "Preacher, my daddy died." . . .

When he said that, you got through to me, Lord. Everybody is worth something to somebody.

Lord, teach me not to judge lest I be judged!

37. *Loving God Is Knowing God*

Through a high powered telescope I saw many times more of your universe than I ever saw before, Lord. The moon swelled; the larger stars quit blinking and took on a steady glow; the ones unseen by the naked eye began to blink. The more I saw, the more I realized I couldn't see. My mind got that squishy feeling that it always gets when it tries to think in areas it was not made for.

Since my mind is incapable of comprehending the universe you have made, it remains unthinkable that I should even attempt to know all about you. Who am *I* to try to prove *you* exist? It seems to be audacity in man that even tries to name you "God."

But this much I know—I can love you and my neighbor

and know the joy of living in doing this. I may not know all about you, Lord. But I know you. And that's enough knowledge to last a lifetime.

38. *Love Changes Things—And People*

Your love surely changes things . . . and people. A mother recently expressed to me her disappointment concerning the girl that her son was about to marry. Admittedly, with the girl's being much taller than he, with her sub-standard education and etiquette, they looked to the outsider like a mis-match.

But they act so differently when you get to know them. They *a c t* like they love each other.

Again, it's your love that counts the most, Lord. The lesson is obvious. Nobody ever marries a common, ordinary person. Love always makes a mate into someone uncommon and extraordinary.

Come to think of it, Lord, maybe that is why the mother felt as she did about her son. She loved him so much that in her eyes he was extraordinary!

What a different world this would be if we loved each other enough to accept the unacceptable, to love the unlovable.

Your love surely changes things . . . and people.

39. *Whom To Please?*

There was a time, Lord, when I thought that being a Christian meant that everybody would love me.

I'll admit, the years have changed this concept. Sometimes it seems that the more good I do, the more enemies I make. Now, mind you, I do not mean that these are enemies in my mind. Thanks to you, Lord, *I* don't have an enemy.

What I mean is: somebody is always misinterpreting what I say, what I do, what I am. Some even disagree over their disagreements about me.

The question is: how much attention should I give to an "enemy's" interpretation of my life?

Somehow you seem to move me to pay less and less attention to man's praises, curses, or whatever. And more and more to your interpretation of my life.

That is the one I am concerned about. That one is eternal!

40. Human Dignity

I've preached for years that our age needs to find human dignity through a better manner of dress. I've talked for a manner of dress that would grace the beauty of womanhood. Instead of prostituting her flesh. And downgrading her soul.

I still preach that ethic, Lord, because it's right.

. . . But then a few days ago I baptized a twenty-four-year-old woman before an average contemporary church congregation. And she was dressed in a miniskirt! It was one of the loveliest, most meaningful baptisms ever. I'll always believe that . . . because it was right.

In her mind she was doing her best, in dress and in spirit.

I look forward to the day of another such confession of faith and baptism.

Meanwhile I'm doing all I can to call for a dress compatible to the best that man can be.

But always holding out an understanding love to those who may not understand.

It's you I'm holding out, Lord.

41. Humility

How right you are, Lord. Humility is a way of life no matter what is one's status.

In recent years astronauts have taken over the national limelight from movie stars and politicians.

Whenever one of them speaks, all of NASA listens and accommodates. Corporation and business officials entertain them regularly. Even the Congress of the United States is all ears when they speak.

This red carpet treatment could spoil any one of them. But I know some who don't let it.

Their regular attendance at worship, work with youth, witnessing of their faith in you, Lord, whether on earth or in orbit around the earth . . . all point to a way of life. A way that smacks of genuine humanity.

They don't realize it, but it looks to us like humility.

"They don't realize it." Oh, yes, Lord, that is the secret of humility. It is not something we get; it's something *you* give.

42. More On Humility

I have talked about how some of our nation's astronauts have learned the way of humility.

Their wives, bless their souls, have learned it too. I don't know who got it from whom. But that's beside the point. Their way of life can be as simple and humble as the local washerwoman's.

Only this week one of them spent a whole day at our "Old Sanctuary" cleaning the floors. There she was on hands and knees scrubbing.

I did not see her. And I'm glad I didn't. Possibly in assuring her that the janitor would take care of the floors, I would have robbed her of a meaningful experience.

The question is still haunting, Lord. Why would she give her time and energy for such a menial task?

. . . Somehow I feel that you had a hand in it somewhere. Surely here is a modern parable that teaches humility.

43. No Self-Pity

I chuckled and I know you did too, Lord. When that seventy-nine-year-old said about herself, "I am poor; I am old; and I am a widow woman. But, she whined, "I'm not a poor, old, widow woman!"

Self-pity is not her downfall. Quite the contrary, she does as much to lift spirits as any person I know. She has done it for others; she's done it for me.

When I feel a bit sorry for myself, just a remembrance of this dear old soul helps to bring me to my senses. And I become in spirit a rich, young servant of man.

With your help, Lord, I hope to do for others what she has done for me.

PART V
ABOUT RANDOM THOUGHTS

44. Prayer

Here's another confession, Lord.

I feel strange every time I open my mouth to pray a prayer. I didn't used to feel this way. But I do now.

I feel unsure of the words. They always seem so completely inadequate. Don't misunderstand me, now. I'm not saying I don't want to pray. Oh, I do want to pray. I do. But when I do, I don't feel I'm saying much.

Now I'm not asking you to make my prayers sound perfect. And above all, I'm not complaining. I just want you to know how inadequate I feel, even as I talk with you now.

No, please don't ever let me fall into the old trap of thinking I am up to proper praying. Knowing the truth of my weakness is good for me.

The next time that I pray a pastoral prayer and someone comes up and says to me, "Oh, that was a perfect prayer, beautifully said," you and I, Lord, will know the truth. The words fall far short of the mark.

But you have accepted me. That's why I believe you accept my prayers.

45. Angels

No one can tell me that angels do not exist, Lord. I

see them every week in hospitals. Dressed in their starched white uniforms these hearty women nurse the sick back to health and relieve the dying of their pain.

I watch one of their ranks carry bedpans of human wastes, clean sores of the diseased, change blood-stained bed sheets, sink medicine-filled needles into sick bodies, wipe perspiration from the forehead of a body racked in pain, receive emergency cases from auto crashes, calmly comfort the hysterical, counsel the neurotic patient . . .

They may be called professionals, Lord. But they are far more than that. They are angels of mercy.

Now I can better understand the answer a nurse gave to a newsman in a tent hospital near the war zone.

He said, "I wouldn't do what you are doing for all the money in the world."

And she answered, "Neither would I."

46. Faith

Lord, if I should ever need proof that man is created by you with eternal potential, I've found a breed of people who offers that evidence. They are the ones who live like they think they'll never die!

They cling to things like they'll have them *forever*.

They talk as if they are creating eternal little empires on the earth.

Now, I don't need such proof of your eternal purpose. Faith in eternal life has been sufficient.

But then maybe it is that faith which helps me see eternal potential in even those who say they don't believe in it.

Whatever the case, Lord, I surely appreciate the sight that faith gives.

47. Table Grace

I said grace again at the dinner table today, Lord. It was one of those "God is great, God is good" varieties that just comes out by habit. And it sounded like a flop to me. But again, maybe those that sound to *me* like a flop might sound to *you* like genuine prayers.

Could it be that when I think I am at my best, I really am at my worst? And when I think I am at my worst in prayer, I am really at my best?

What I think I'll do just now is: quit thinking whether I am or am not talking with you in the right theological terms, voice inflections, etc.

I think I'll just listen.

Amen!

48. God's Love

There's so much I do not understand about the Bible, Lord. But those scriptures don't really bother me. It's this kind of simple truth that is easy to understand, but hard to live by: "You shall love the Lord your God with all your heart and your neighbor as yourself."

Now I can love you, Lord. You've never done anything but help me. And I find it rather easy to love mankind in general. But some of these neighbors that live next door, that I work with, that I go to church with . . . Lord God, they are awful!

One won't speak to me.

One has spread false rumors.

One acts like a self-righteous saint.

It's a cinch, Lord, that I cannot love these individuals *because* they are the wrong kind of people. But *in spite of* their ways, I'll try to love them.

In spite of! Come to think about it, it's the in-spite-of love that you have toward me.

Lord, be merciful to me, a sinner!

49. *Profanity*

I went to the community hardware store this morning. And discovered that its proprietor had died. A wreath of white carnations hung on the door in his memory.

This man in life had been one of the most profane creatures I have ever known. His tongue belched curses profusely. Profanity for him was not a matter of using a few bad words. It was his language.

Now, however, it is not his profanity that bothers me. But my negligence in never once talking with him about you, Lord. He probably never knew that I was a minister of the gospel. I know I never told him.

The bother is: I'm not sure whose profanity was worse, his or mine. He profaned your name by using it disrespectfully. I profaned it by not using it at all in his presence.

Lord, forgive me.

Maybe he asked forgiveness too.

Oh, I hope so. I really liked the old cuss.

50. A Sermon

We ordinarily think of sermons as spoken discourses.

But I saw one in a picture today, Lord. The picture was taken by a pilot friend who had flown a party of fishermen to Lake Novillow, a placid sky-blue lake cupped among the heights of the Sierra Madres in Mexico. They were fishing over what was once a small valley town with a mountain creek flowing through it. The canyon had been dammed leaving one of the best bass fishing lakes in all of North America.

And now comes the surprise . . . and the sermon.

Right in the middle of the lake protrudes the tower of an old church. The best fishing was done through the tower!

My, how things do change. Where there once worshipped a people who would eat only fish on Friday, now was the spawning ground for fish. Where the bell rope was once pulled to signal mass, now the line of a fisherman jerks to signal bass. Where once filtered through the voices of worshippers below, now there is silence. No sound except the slight splash of the water against the belfry tower, which only serves to accentuate the deafening silence of the depths.

It says so much, Lord.

What is the world doing to the church today?

What has time done to the church during these 2000 years?

We've done worse to the church than fish on Sunday!

Nowhere can we go and escape the lesson of the cross.

Christ comes through the unexpected. That picture

is a sermon, Lord. And even now, messages are still coming through.

51. *Up There*

In this space age, Lord, I've been telling folks that you are not "up there," that you are deep, deep inside us. I believe this.

But every time I read the prayer to you composed by Gordon Cooper during his Faith 7 flight, I have to back up a bit and admit that "up there" you surely work on a fellow's insides.

Judging from the spirit of his words, Gordo surely must have had a wonderful time with you "up there." But why didn't the cosmonaut "see" you?

I believe now I know. If he didn't "have his feet on the ground" down here, in faith, he would miss you "up there."

To these men of the faith you are big down here, Lord. But how much bigger you are to them "up there"!

Maybe that's a clue to your nature. The more we see of your universe, the bigger you become. And stronger is our faith.

Footnote: Gordon Cooper's handwritten prayer rests behind glass in the Narthex of Seabrook Methodist Church, where he is a member.

52. *The Devil*

How subtly do our minds evade the truth, Lord.

Recently I talked with a man, who was most upset about his little son digging a hole in the back yard while muttering, "Come out of there, Devil, I know you are down there." This father was visibly shaken because he knew that there was no thing down there called the Devil.

But it is my experience that the son was closer to the truth than many adults. There are forces in control of maniacal actions of men that cannot be analyzed away as inconsequential factors.

Lord, some who act like the Devil, don't believe in "him."

I accept the truth that there are negative forces loose in the world that would have me hate those I love, cheat my neighbor, and not even believe in you.

This tyranny of evil can be called anything. But for lack of better words I just hang a mask on this evil and call "him" the Devil. Talking to this elusive nothingness that would take away all meaning to life in personal terms such as "Devil" or "Satan" seems absolutely permissable. In fact the terms seem necessary.

Whenever I am tempted to spitefully misuse those I love, I know that really I don't want to do this, that something is about to get me into trouble. That something is the Devil. You said it yourself, Lord.

"Get thee behind me, Satan."

Who am I to think that I or anybody else could improve the term that you have put upon the head of this prince of the darkness of this world?

The devil!

53. *The Commandments*

Thank you, Lord, for the Ten Commandments. And above all, thank you for the eleventh one, the one that instructs us to love our neighbors and you with all our strength. If it weren't for that one, we wouldn't be able to keep the other commandments in a fulfilling kind of way.

Your love in our actions, as we keep the commandments, is a must.

But, oh Lord, how we weak humans use the commandments. You remember the young high school couple for whom I read the marriage vows last year. Her pregnancy was justifiied in their minds because they loved each other. And I believe they did love each other very much. But they are divorced now, with no desire on the part of either to come together. And the baby is caught in the squeeze.

How they needed to keep the commandment to not commit adultery! Which would have meant fighting the urge for physical love-making. Because of a deeper love and respect for each other.

This I do know for myself, the commandments help to keep me out of situations, where, if I permitted myself the temptation, I might justify wrong actions through a "love" that is not you, Lord. That reason alone is sufficient enough for me to say that I need the commandments.

And with them I need your spirit of love.

54. Lord

I used to wonder why some people called you Jehovah, others called you Allah, others called you God, and others called you Being-itself, Lord, and so on.

I don't wonder anymore. How could any human

word describe you? Indeed, it is man's egotism that calls you "he" instead of "she." "It" might even be more appropriate in talking about you. But "it" connotes a thing. And you're more than that. You are more than anything that exists in this life. You are the Creator of all things that exist in this life.

Now I understand why you described yourself upon one occasion, "I Am That I Am." You were being before we or anything was. Our words describe this world, not your life.

I know that even the word "Lord" is inadequate in addressing you, Lord. But I use it because my words are all I have.

Anyway, you know what I mean when I say "Lord." As long as you get that message, even if it were possible, the perfect words couldn't do more.

55. The Rainbow

Lord, you didn't have a more dedicated follower than I when those storms caught us from all sides. The airplane wasn't flying through the air. It was bouncing, lurching, sliding, sinking, rising. To say the least it was shaky. My put-on calm look did not fool anybody, certainly not myself.

And then within a little while everything settled down as the clouds began to disperse and sunlight began to filter through. At which time my daughter cried out, "Look, daddy, we're in the middle of a rainbow!"

Sure enough, below us and to the side was a completely circled rainbow. And in its soft middle was the shadow of our plane.

Vividly brought to mind is our faith that the beauties of forgiveness, peace, and comfort follow the storms of guilt, fear, and grief just as surely as the rainbow follows the storms of nature. There could never be the joys of forgiveness, peace, and comfort without the preceding storms.

We never enjoy the stormy times of life, Lord. But if they have to come, it surely is good to know that a rainbow is coming up soon.

56. Things

What's going on around here, Lord?

A floor joist on the long, high porch across the front of our country cabin has broken. And the porch is sagging. Before the house is completed, some of it is rotting away!

I look around me and see deterioration everywhere. Those are new drapes on the windows. But how long did they lay on the store's shelf before they got to this place? How long will it be before the last washing leaves them in tatters?

How long will the chair I'm sitting in hold anybody up? When will it crumple due to the fatigue of just being around awhile?

Oh, yes. That's the second air conditioner there in the wall. I wonder where the first one is now? The last time I saw it, a truck was hauling it to a dump somewhere.

And so it goes. Everywhere my mind turns I see transistoriness. Whoops, I looked in a mirror. And saw myself — a thing among things.

Lord, I feel like all creation is giving away right under me. Everything ends up as dirt. And I feel I'm on a landslide!

I asked, "What's going on around here, Lord?" I don't really want the answer to that question. I see what's going on. I see everything going on into oblivion.

What I really have is not a question, but a request:

"Change and decay, in all around I see.

Oh, thou who changest not—

Abide with me."

57. The Lord's Supper

For many years now I have administered the sacrament of your supper, Lord. It's always meant so much to me. Your presence is truly there.

Men have tried for ages to create a doctrine explaining what happens when we take the elements of bread and wine. Some say that they are actually eating your body, that the elements are you. Others say that the elements are "just" symbols. As if to imply that they just "stand for" your presence.

Lord, I believe that they *are* symbols that indicate your real presence. This must be what's happening because I sense you near us in it all.

Just like a lonely soldier's picture of his wife or girl friend "brings" her spirit right there with him, so the wine and bread are used as means of bringing you, Lord, right in the middle of a congregation of worshippers. The soldier speaks to the picture and says, "I love you." He really feels her near him. We "feed on him in our hearts." Devotedly the soldier holds her picture and proclaims, "That *is* my wife." In devotion to you, Lord, we hold the elements as the words are proclaimed, "This *is* the body—this *is* the blood of our Lord Jesus Christ—."

Yes, Lord, these *are* symbols, not "just" symbols. Through them we know you are present.

Every word we speak on any occasion, every object we see anywhere, every action we do anytime are symbols for something. But none is more meaningful than the symbols of your Supper, Lord. We hold those symbols, we look at them, we think about them, and there you are, Lord! With us! Then the Supper becomes Communion with you. It is a Supper for the soul.

58. *Dialogue*

Words—we can't do without them, Lord.

But sometimes they are hard to do with.

That fellow called Socrates and others after him claimed that understanding comes through dialogue. Lord, I heard two theologians dialogue heatedly for a whole year. And I'm not sure either truly got over his points to the other. And understanding seemed more remote in the end than in the beginning.

Now this is the way it seems to me, Lord. Dialogue can lead to understanding only after understanding is established between the talkers. Men may talk and talk and talk and never understand each other. Then again they may talk and talk and finally something happens and understanding results.

Now what is it that happens, Lord? I believe the answer is you. You happen to get hold of one or both of the talkers. And they begin to witness, to tell the good news they understand. Then the dialogue which follows that is something to behold.

Maybe that's why the "dialogue" in these talks with you, Lord, leads to a wider understanding between us. Something has already happened to me which is too deep for words.

"For we know not what we should pray for as we ought: but the Spirit itself maketh intercession for us with groanings which cannot be uttered."

Romans 8:26

59. A Change

I've often said, "I want to get away where I can't hear a sound." But come to think of it, Lord, I don't want that. I just want to hear different sounds.

"I want to go to the peace and quiet of the woods," have been my words.

But it's not the peace and quiet of the woods I want. It is quietness *with* the noises of nature. It is silence broken by the croaking of a bull frog, the hoot of the hoot-owl, the ka-plunk of a pebble in a calm lake, the caw of the crow in the distance, the whh-whun-whia of the whipporwill in the middle of a hushing sunset—it's music.

Some folks feel that a change of scenery is adequate. That's good, but there's more that goes with a change of scenery. And that is a change of sounds.

I suppose if I lived only in the country the sight and the sounds of the big city would be a welcome change.

But that's not our situation. We are so urbanized that

our dog has to have proper room temperature and a
sheet to cover up with when he sleeps.

So the change of sight and sounds we look for comes
from the country. When we get there, the winds whistling
through the tall trees, the bass jumping and splashing
in the lake, the bull bellowing, the horses whinnying
or the John Deere tractor popping in the far distance
never let us down.

It's just what we are looking for. And they seem to
know it—their sounds and sights are so clear, so full of
life. If only they could know how much we appreciate
what they give us.

But no, that wouldn't do. Then we might credit them.
When you deserve the praise.

Thank you, Lord, for our companions of nature and
for the ability to appreciate and enjoy them.

PART VI
ABOUT HAPPY TIMES

60. Time

I don't know what kind of clock you put in our brain when you created us. But for sure there's one there. At least, this is my experience.

In the metropolis, everything goes so fast—cars, trains, airplanes. We are in those conveyances. Which means that we are going fast.

In this environment time goes fast, so fast. Lord, it's like getting up, gulping a bit of food, stepping outside, and just turning around and coming back in, gulping food, and going to bed. It's rush, rush, rush. And we feel it all over.

But here with the rolling rural hills of East Texas things slow down. My speech even slows down to match the tempo of my neighbors. Normally I don't even wear a watch here. Suppertime comes at the "time" everything is wound up, not when the clock strikes 6:00 p.m. Or whatever time we eat in the city.

Oh, the clock on the mantle may strike all night long. But that's just to awaken us enough to know where we are!

For a fact I live "longer" when I'm here in the country. And if you see fit, Lord, to bring me here periodically throughout the years ahead, I'll be an old, old man when you summon me home.

I understand time really "goes slow" there, and it stretches on and on and on.

61. Happiness

Lord, I read where the psalmist said, "Behold, this is the day that the Lord has made. Rejoice and be glad in it."

I honestly feel like I can do that today. And it is a good feeling. I am happy. And I haven't done a thing to make myself feel this way.

It does not really make sense. — My father is just a breath from death, the doctors say. And mother carries a cross heavier than his. She's nurse, housewife, wage earner. Right now I have four parishioners in hospitals; two are critically ill. And the funeral of another is pending. — And I am happy today.

It defies logic.

But, Lord, I've noticed that this is the way you work. I do not understand how you do it. And I'm not asking to understand. I'm just grateful.

This much I know: my happiness won't hurt these dear friends and loved ones whose burdens seem heavier than mine.

Thank you, Lord, from everybody for anybody's happiness.

62. Freedom

Look at those faces, Lord — two hundred of them. These men have been caught. And they look that way.

In a silent, anxious, controlled, blank expression they show that the one burning desire is freedom.

They are behind bars. Which accounts for the trapped look common to them all.

I've talked to men like this before. And I know their greatest desire — freedom.

The "bars" and "barbed wire" may be the physical limits of a prison, or the lack of funds to travel which keeps a person close to home, or a limited time to go anywhere, or the natural boundary of a country, or physical disabilities. Every person is a prisoner in some way. He has his limitations.

Since everybody is confined in some way, freedom must be more than spatial. I've known some folks who never leave the farm, the ghetto, the apartments. Some actually have less space than the prison farm. But freedom for them comes in their not being forced inside boundaries.

Since freedom is a thing of the mind, maybe some of these inmates have discovered the wide-open spaces of the soul.

Come to think of it, Lord, a few of them did talk with courage and conviction about what you have done for them.

Freedom inside the small confines of prison! It's a miracle!

63. *Prisoners*

An interesting thing has happened, Lord. Something that I had not planned on. I talked to you about the 200 prison faces who had lost their freedom in society.

Lo and behold I now get behind the pulpit and look
into the glaring faces of as many people in my own
congregation who have that same look. They have lost
their freedom.

Some are prisoners of their own selves. Unable to love
others, they feel cut off.

Their situation seems more tragic than the prisoners
of civil authorities. Because they don't recognize the
wall of indifference, the barbed wire of resentment,
the fence of pride that surround their lives, which
keep them from getting out to others and keep others
from getting in with them.

They look like their very souls are calling for freedom.

I sometimes feel the call myself. In those moments
my soul cries for release from the frustrations of fears
and resentments against those whom I love the most.

My soul finds that freedom every time that I admit that I am hasty, if not wrong, in my judgments.
Truth hurts, Lord, but like you said, it frees.

"Know the truth and the truth will make you free."

64. A Worship Service

O Lord, how I wish my own congregation enjoyed a
worship service as much as those prisoners in this maximum security unit of the Texas prison system.

I was astonished to hear those negro prisoners singing verses in Spanish. How they enjoyed the effort!

And the hearty Amens during the preaching did
something for me that I cannot explain. Except to say
that their reactions made the sermon exciting for me!

And then during the final moments, with heads bowed, at least fifty hands were eased silently into the air, signalling that Christ's way to spiritual freedom was being walked. The response was electrifying!

And then the dozen who waited patiently yet anxiously for counsel and prayer showed that the response was real.

I know one thing. I'll be a better preacher for having been there.

Maybe that's the answer for my congregation. Maybe they've been waiting for me to get enthusiastic about something.

If that's the case, Lord, it won't be any longer. I'm ready and rarin' to go.

65. The Pot Plants

It takes so little to make some folks happy. The folks I am thinking about, Lord, are old folks. They don't want new homes, cars, clothes, gadgets. Any day they will settle for a kind word, a ready smile. Anything more is a bonus.

And even the bonus seems so little in comparison to most of our demands.

In our community home for elderly citizens some youth brought small potted plants to the golden aged. One non-blooming plant to a pot set in each room, some on windows, others on special tables, and each day some were transported from darkened corners of inside rooms to a sun porch. The plants were petted and meticulously cared for in every way. Their proud owners watched them closely as they stretched in growth and yawned into large blossoms.

The plants seemed to do just what was expected of them. They seemed to communicate the idea that older people are as worthwhile as anybody to this world. This message didn't come by observing the plants, however, but by watching the bright eyes of the proud owners. Behind those eyes were happy souls.

66. It's Me And Thee

Right now, it's just "me and thee," Lord.

But it hasn't been this way all day.

At 11:00 this A.M. it was "me and thee" and a host of people at a funeral. It was good to feel needed at such a time of crises in people's lives. And you were the Comforter of us all.

And then I got in my airplane as quickly as the Chapel service ended and flew to a 1:00 P.M. Church Renewal meeting 200 miles away.

At 5:00 P.M. I landed at our restful retreat in the rolling hills of East Texas.

And now, again, Lord, it's just "me and thee."

It's so quiet and peaceful. I hear no noises—only sounds. On the shores of the lake only 50 feet away are bull frogs answering each other in rhythm with deep bass voices; crickets are their competition; a timber wolf howls from across the creek and in the distance an owl hoots, nature's way of saying "all is well."

And that is the way I feel as I close my eyes after this long day.

Good night, Lord.

67. They Changed

Nobody was trying to impress you with that baptism at the Worship Service this morning, Lord. But knowing you, I believe you were impressed.

There they stood—Donny and Judy. As a child Judy had heard about you. But Donny, as intelligent a man as I've ever met, didn't know you. He didn't even know about you!

But, then, in a way he did know about you. In fact he was struggling with you. He wanted a love for and from Judy that was sacrificial, forgiving, respectful, the whole bit. And, like I told him, that Love is you!

Remember, I prayed "O Force of Divine Love" with him. You knew we were talking to you, Lord, even though I did not call you "Lord" or "God." I know you knew because we three felt your overpowering presence.

Through tears Donny accepted your way of life, on your terms, by saying, "I'll buy that." And they were forgiven.

Right now Donny's back at a local night club, doing the only job he knows. As a solo musician he is fingering a piano or strumming a guitar for his bleary-eyed audience.

But his spirit has changed the environment. In many instances, the loose attitude toward sex still prevails, tobacco smoke and alcohol odors hang heavily in the air; and sporadically fights break out. But the environment has changed—because Donny's changed. These "lost" people have found someone they can talk to. And one by one, one today and one next week, they are learning that Donny's got something. Donny's got you.

Through Donny's witness maybe mothers will go home to children, husbands will go home to wives.

I remember Donny's last visit to my office. I went home from that encounter with a lifted spirit. I am his pastor, and he helped me!

The names Donny and Judy are fictitious; the persons are real.

68. *Vocation*

People wouldn't understand. But I know you understand, Lord, why I get such a bang out of being with these astronauts.

They are not one bit better than anybody else. And the ones I know would be embarrassed to know that anybody thought that of them. Or especially thought that they thought that of themselves!

But they are flyers. That's why I especially enjoy their companionship.

After spending last evening with two astronauts, both of whom have been honored by our nation for their accomplishments in outer space, I must admit that in my mind there are very few jobs more appealing than the work these men are doing.

But as I listened, again I was made aware of the wonders of my own calling. As exciting and wondrous as the beauties of space are, there is hardly any comparison to that joyous experience of helping one to see the beauties of the Christian faith. And to choose that way of life.

In your sight, Lord, the first man standing on the moon will be a much, much less significant event than a humble man standing at the altar of your church.

Now, I recognize this fact. And nothing could shake my awareness of the truth of it. But every time one of my flying friends goes out there, I get that "left behind" feeling. A feeling not so bad when you consider I've got the greatest calling in the world. While they link up the planets, I am linking up men with you, Lord. It's an eternal orbit around your life, your will. Nothing counts more than that.

69. *Good Show!*

Lord, I know you had a ball at the local dog show in a neighbor's back yard.

There they were, ten dogs (and some were really doggy!), eighteen kids, and parents.

The dogs looked their best. Our daughter's white chihuahua, "Tiger," had gone through the ordeal of four baths for the occasion. And surprisingly enough, the dogs were fairly well mannered, with possibly some sensing that they were on review. They strutted their stuff.

The children watched the dogs closely.

But it was apparent that the parents were not eyeing the dogs so much as they were observing the children. Especially when the little judges gave out the ribbons. The dignity of the occasion was not denied in any sense.

Tiger's second place ribbon was something to behold. Two roughly snipped pieces of red ribbon pasted onto a small cardboard wrapped in foil, with "second place" scrawled on it in a manner indicating much effort went into the penmanship—made up the trophy.

Without a doubt the show the children put on was, to the parents, better than the dog's.

But I have a sneaky feeling that you were provided the best show of all by the parents. Who stood as one body, peeking out the kitchen window. In those faces was an amount of pride, balanced by genuine gratitude, for their children. They were overjoyed at the joy they saw in their offspring.

But nobody had a ringside seat like you, Lord. There were your dogs, your children, your parents of those children. They were all completely being themselves in a good kind of way. In a world where there is war, murder, hatred galore, it must please you to see such a grand drama.

We've caused you so many heartaches, that such a drama of innocence must indeed be a relief for you.

It was a good show, Lord. I hope you have many more.

70. Worldly Things

What a lesson you taught me, Lord!

I remember the time in my ministry where I actually felt a kind of contempt for the things of this world. Worldly things were sinful, bad, evil.

And then, wham! In a despair so shaking I felt cut off from the world.

A day before this despair struck, I would have never believed I would have prayed the prayer I prayed, not once, but many, many times during the depression.

How long, how long, O Lord, I prayed for a feeling for this world. For the enjoyment of a football game, for the thrill of driving a car. It didn't have to be new. Just knowing I was driving the car was sufficient. For the taste of food, for the feel of clothes on my back. For life in this world.

I prayed earnestly for it all, Lord. You took your time (which undoubtedly was part of my test). But you gave it all to me. Life as a whole now is exciting beyond words. Driving cars, flying planes, preaching, viewing movies, writing, fishing, visiting—

Right now, this world is my home. And I love it. Thanks to the Source of Love. Thanks to you, Lord.

71. A Birthday Party

Tonight's birthday party was the most unusual I ever attended.

Friends gathered around cake 'n all to celebrate the young mother's third birthday.

Third birthday, Lord! It had been three years to the day since she had a drink of alcohol.

At three years of age our daughter was not nearly so happy as this three-year-old alcoholic was at hers.

Her husband may forget the date of her birth into the world. But she has informed him that he had better not forget her birthday since rebirth of the soul, since she got back her life by giving herself to you.

The next time I sing "Happy Birthday" to anyone, Lord, I'll think of her. I'll think of you. Your birthday parties are the best.

72. Christ

You're a powerful mystery, Lord. Just the calling of your name encourages, inspires, lifts the spirit of man.

I saw this happen one day as I was waiting for the elevator on the fifth floor of a hospital. Standing beside me was an elderly lady who looked like she was in the need of a good word. What I said triggered a conversation that still makes me stand in awed wonder at the power of your name.

I simply asked: "What would we do without Christ?"

That simple, straightforward question opened a floodgate that spilled conversation from that moment on the fifth floor, throughout the elevator ride down to the first floor, and even out into the street where she finally broke off by saying, "Thank you for talking to me!"—

My part of the conversation amounted to one question!

But a question that affirms faith in you, Lord.

Similar situations will present themselves again and again. Keep me on my toes, Lord. That I will be ready to speak.

And willing to listen.

39441